CONTENTS

WALL OF SNOW

After days of heavy snowfall on the mountain, sunshine warms the air. Suddenly a huge slab of snow loosens. The wall of snow slides down the slope. Run! It's an **avalanche**!

THE WORLD'S WORST NATURAL DISASTERS

THE WORLD'S WORST AVALANCHES

by Tracy Nelson Maurer

Raintree is an imprint of Capstone Global Library Limited, a company incorporated in England and Wales having its registered office at 264 Banbury Road, Oxford, OX2 7DY – Registered company number: 6695582

www.raintree.co.uk
myorders@raintree.co.uk

Edited by Gena Chester
Designed by Juliette Peters
Original illustrations © Capstone Global Library Limited 2019
Picture research by Jo Miller
Production by Tori Abraham
Originated by Capstone Global Library Ltd
Printed and bound in India

ISBN 978 1 4747 7122 1 (hardback)
22 21 20 19 18
10 9 8 7 6 5 4 3 2 1

ISBN 978 1 4747 7126 9 (paperback)
23 22 21 20 19
10 9 8 7 6 5 4 3 2 1

British Library Cataloguing in Publication Data
A full catalogue record for this book is available from the British Library.

Acknowledgements
We would like to thank the following for permission to reproduce photographs: AP Images: Str, 16–17; Dreamstime: Brett Pelletier, 26; Getty Images: AAron Ontiveroz/Contributor, 24–25, Jack Fletcher/Contributor, 14–15, Library of Congress/Contributor, 10–11, Roberto Schmidt/Staff, 18–19, SHAH MARAI, 12–13; Mary Evans Picture Library: Illustrated London News Ltd, 20–21; Newscom: Danita Delimont Photography, 27; Shutterstock: leonello calvetti, Cover, 3, 31, My Good Images, Cover, 4–5, Piotr Snigorski, 29; SuperStock: Clickalps SRLs/age fotostock VFI-2792927, 22–23, Exactostock-1598, 8–9, World History Archive, 6–7. Design Elements: Shutterstock: Ivana Milic, Lysogor Roman, xpixe.l

Ice, rock, **debris** and snow are all types of avalanches.

avalanche mass of snow, rocks, ice or soil that slides down a mountain slope; avalanches are also called snow slides

debris piles of rock fragments and loose, natural materials

ANIMAL DISASTER

Location:
The Alps, Italy

Date:
218 BC

Lives Lost:
About 18,000

#####
#####
#####
###
_____

= 1 thousand people

More than 2,000 years ago, a North African army was crossing into Italy through the **Alps**. Horses and elephants carried their gear. The elephants' heavy footsteps on fresh snow set off avalanches. About 18,000 men died.

FACT Avalanches happen for many reasons. Rapidly warming temperatures and extreme weather are common causes.

Alps large mountain range in Europe

DANGER ZONE

Location:
Andermatt,
Switzerland

Date:
Winter of
1950–1951

Lives Lost:
240

#

= 1 hundred people

Andermatt, Switzerland, faced heavy snowfall during the winter of 1950–1951. The weather caused a series of avalanches. On 20 January, six avalanches roared down the Alps. They caused massive destruction and killed 240 people.

FACT Since 1936, more than 2,000 people have died in avalanches in Switzerland.

THE WORST AVALANCHE IN THE USA

Location:
Wellington,
Washington, USA

Date:
1 March 1910

Lives Lost:
At least 96

#####
#####

= ten people

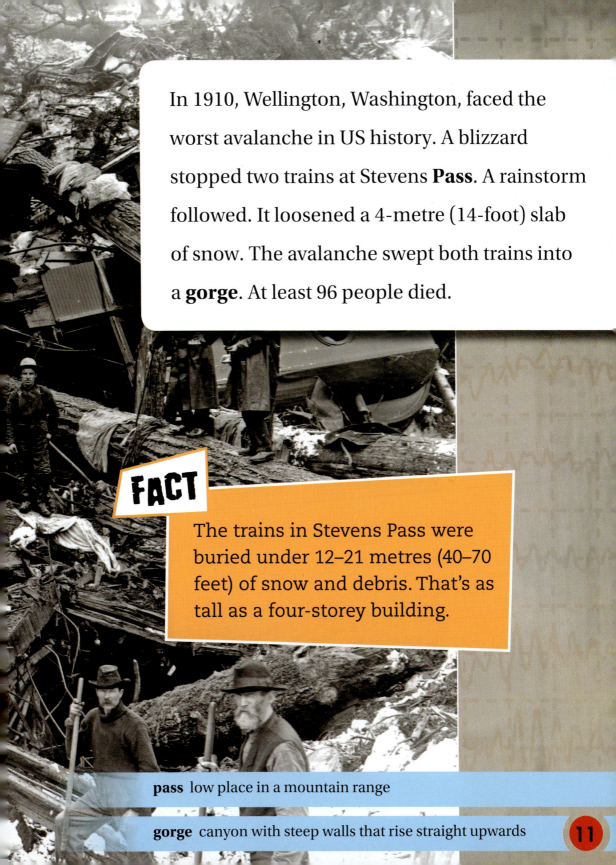

In 1910, Wellington, Washington, faced the worst avalanche in US history. A blizzard stopped two trains at Stevens **Pass**. A rainstorm followed. It loosened a 4-metre (14-foot) slab of snow. The avalanche swept both trains into a **gorge**. At least 96 people died.

FACT

The trains in Stevens Pass were buried under 12–21 metres (40–70 feet) of snow and debris. That's as tall as a four-storey building.

pass low place in a mountain range

gorge canyon with steep walls that rise straight upwards

11

RISKY ROADWAY

Location:
Salang Pass,
Afghanistan

Date:
9 February 2010

Lives Lost:
More than 170

##

= 1 hundred people

On 9 February 2010, 17 avalanches rumbled through Salang Pass in Afghanistan. The snow buried cars, lorries and buses. It also clogged a tunnel. Thousands of people were trapped inside. More than 170 people died.

FACT

Rescue workers managed to save around 3,000 people in Salang Pass.

KILLER ICE

Location:
Andes Mountains, Peru

Date:
31 May 1970

Lives Lost:
About 25,000

#####
#####
#####
#####
#####

= 1 thousand people

In 1962, an ice avalanche on Mount Huascarán, Peru, destroyed several villages. At least 3,500 people died. Eight years later, an avalanche of rock and snow struck the same area. The disaster killed about 25,000 people.

FACT

The 1970 avalanche ripped down the mountain at 210–280 kilometres (130–174 miles) per hour.

RUSSIAN RUIN

Location:
North Ossetia,
Russia

Date:
20 September
2002

Lives Lost:
More than 100

= 1 hundred people

In 2002, near North Ossetia, Russia, a large chunk of ice broke off a **glacier**. It sped down a mountain, starting an avalanche. The ice, water and rock buried the town of Nizhny Karmadon. More than 100 people died.

FACT

Another glacier broke off near North Ossetia in 1902. It caused a smaller avalanche than the 2002 disaster.

glacier huge moving body of ice that flows down a mountain slope or across a polar region

NO ESCAPE

Location:
Mount Everest,
Nepal

Date:
25 April 2015

Lives Lost:
At least 19

#####
#####
#####
####

= 1 person

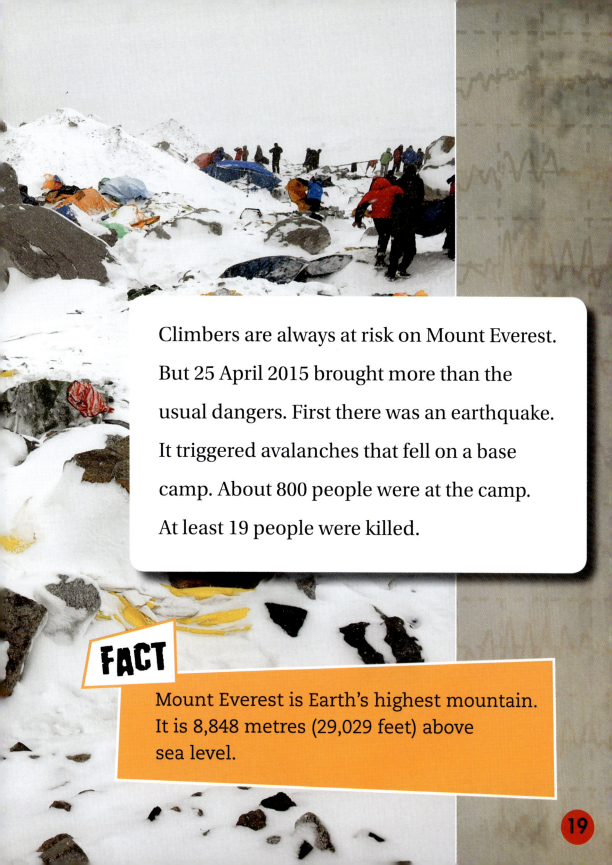

Climbers are always at risk on Mount Everest. But 25 April 2015 brought more than the usual dangers. First there was an earthquake. It triggered avalanches that fell on a base camp. About 800 people were at the camp. At least 19 people were killed.

FACT

Mount Everest is Earth's highest mountain. It is 8,848 metres (29,029 feet) above sea level.

AVALANCHE ATTACKS

Location:
Tyrolean Alps,
Italy

Date:
Winter of
1916–1917

Lives Lost:
About 18,000

\#\#\#\#\#
\#\#\#\#\#
\#\#\#\#\#
\#\#\#

\# = 1 thousand people

During World War I (1914–1918), Italian and Austrian armies in the Alps used avalanches like bombs. **Explosives** and heavy snow triggered a series of avalanches one winter. Around 18,000 soldiers were killed by the snow.

FACT

Bodies caught in avalanches during World War I were still being found 80 years later.

HERE, THEN GONE

Location:
Plurs, Switzerland

Date:
4 September
1618

Lives Lost:
Between 1,500
and 2,500

-
###

= 1 thousand people

The village of Plurs, Switzerland, once sat in the shade of a mountain. The town disappeared in one day. A powerful avalanche swept away everything in its path. Between 1,500 and 2,500 people died.

FACT

Only one building survived the Plurs avalanche. Today it is surrounded by orchards and farmland.

23

PARK RANGER RESCUE

Location:
Cameron Pass,
Colorado, USA

Date:
2 March 2013

Lives Lost:
1

#
_____

= 1 person

Four skiers were in Colorado's Cameron Pass when an avalanche hit. Two, Alex White and Joe Philpott, were buried in the snow. Philpott did not survive. Park rangers eventually found White buried. They dug for three hours and pulled him out alive!

FACT

Most avalanche victims survive if they are dug out within 15 minutes. White only had a 1 per cent chance of survival.

Alex White

AVALANCHE PROTECTION

Avalanches happen in all mountain areas. To help protect people and towns, officials cause avalanches on purpose. That way they can control where snow flows so it causes less damage.

FACT

Some towns have built avalanche **barriers** from wood, metal or concrete.

barrier bar, fence or other object that prevents things from entering an area

SNOW SAFETY

Skiers, hikers and snowmobilers should check snow conditions often. These tips can help you if you're caught in an avalanche:

1. Move your arms as if you're swimming to the surface.
2. Shout out so that people nearby know you're being swept away.
3. If buried, cup your hands over your mouth to create an air pocket for breathing.
4. If buried, poke your arms, a pole or anything above the snow to alert rescuers.

GLOSSARY

Alps large mountain range in Europe

avalanche large mass of ice, snow or earth that suddenly moves down the side of a mountain

barrier bar, fence or other object that prevents things from entering an area

debris piles of rock fragments and loose, natural materials

explosive weapon designed to blow up after reaching its target

glacier huge moving body of ice that flows down a mountain slope or across a polar region

gorge canyon with steep walls that rise straight upwards

pass low place in a mountain range

FIND OUT MORE

BOOKS

Can We Protect People from Natural Disasters? (Earth Debates), Catherine Chambers (Raintree, 2015)

Daring Avalanche Rescues (Rescued!), Amy Waeschle (Raintree, 2018)

Landslides and Avalanches (Natural Disasters), Louise and Richard Spilsbury (Wayland, 2010)

Surviving in the Wilderness (Extreme Survival), Michael Hurley (Raintree, 2012)

WEBSITES

www.bbc.co.uk/schools/gcsebitesize/ geography/glacial_landscapes/avalanches_ rev1.shtml
Learn more about the causes of avalanches.

www.dkfindout.com/uk/earth/mountains
Find out about Earth's mountains.

COMPREHENSION QUESTIONS

1. Name three things that can cause an avalanche.

2. How could an avalanche happen in the summer?

3. Why is it important to cup your hands over your mouth if you become buried in snow?

INDEX